# FIREFIGHTING IN BRISTOL 1877-1974

*An Illustrated History*

# FIREFIGHTING IN BRISTOL 1877-1974

*An Illustrated History*

## DENNIS HILL

TEMPUS

*Front cover:* Bristol Fire Brigade's horse-drawn Magirus turntable
ladder and Shand Mason self-propelled steamer at a fire at Messrs
Morley & Sons, rag, rope and metal merchants, in Fairfax Street,
16 July 1913. The turntable ladder, supplied by John Morris in 1908,
had a working height of 72ft. It did much good work during its
years of service, but became obsolete as self-propelled motor versions
were developed. (Fred Little Collection)

*Frontispiece:* A lunchtime fire on 16 February 1948 that broke out
in the stage area of Bristol's Hippodrome Theatre spread rapidly to
a nearby warehouse. A senior fire officer called for reinforcements
on seeing the smoke as he approached the fire. Total attendance was
nine pumps, two turntable ladders and a fireboat. Twenty-one jets
were used to tackle the fire. Firemen Seward and Hooper are on the
turntable ladders. (Ron Cook)

First published 2007

Tempus Publishing Limited
The Mill, Brimscombe Port,
Stroud, Gloucestershire, GL5 2QG
www.tempus-publishing.com

© Dennis Hill, 2007

The right of Dennis Hill to be identified as the Author
of this work has been asserted in accordance with the
Copyrights, Designs and Patents Act 1988.

British Library Cataloguing in Publication Data.
A catalogue record for this book is available from the British Library.

ISBN 978 07524 4090 3

Typesetting and origination by Tempus Publishing Limited.
Printed in Great Britain.

# Contents

# Acknowledgements

I am most grateful to all who have freely allowed photographs to be reproduced in this publication. Wherever possible, acknowledgement has been given to the source of copyright material.

Many of the photographs were taken by Bristol Fire Brigade photographers and I wish to record my thanks to Kevin Pearson MA MCGI MIFireE, Chief Fire Officer/Chief Executive of Avon Fire & Rescue Service, for giving permission to use them.

# Bibliography

Bristol Fire Brigade, Annual Reports of the Chief Fire Officer (Bristol City Council, 1949–1974)

Bristol Fire Brigade, *Report of Fire at Regent Oil Installation, Royal Edward Dock, Avonmouth, Bristol* (Bristol City Council, 1951)

HM Stationery Office, *Report of the Formal Investigation into the Explosion at M. & M. Mart Garage, Ashley Road, Bristol* (1952)

Blackstone G.V., CBE, GM, *A History of the British Fire Service* (Routledge & Kegan Paul, London, 1957)

Winstone R., *Bristol Blitzed* (1973)

Hill D., *Bristol Fire Brigade 1877-1974 An Illustrated History* (Redcliffe Press Ltd, 1999)

# Introduction

Prior to 1877 fire protection in Bristol was provided by six insurance companies – the Sun, Liverpool & London & Globe, Royal, Imperial, West of England and Norwich Union, each running a small brigade of retained firemen equipped with manual fire engines. Bristol Constabulary, established in 1836, operated a limited amount of firefighting and rescue equipment, including wheeled escape ladders.

The inadequacies of the arrangements were highlighted dramatically by two fires in 1876. One, in a group of warehouses, caused immense damage and led to huge insurance claims. The other, in domestic property, claimed the lives of three members of the same family. Five insurance companies disbanded their brigades and handed over their equipment to Bristol City Council, who formed a police fire brigade with twelve constables under a superintendent. A horse-drawn, steam-powered fire engine was purchased from Merryweather & Sons Ltd of Greenwich, London, and the new brigade commenced its duties on 1 July 1877. The Imperial Fire Office kept their firemen and manual engine to attend out-of-town fires.

Alterations were made to the central police station in Bridewell Street to accommodate the new brigade. Firefighting equipment was also kept at other police stations in the city. The number of firemen barely increased in twenty years, and when it did it was largely in response to major extensions to the city's boundaries, particularly in 1897 when the number was doubled to twenty-eight. By then Bristol's population was more than 320,000 compared with 207,000 in 1877. The river police manned a steam-powered fire float purchased in 1885.

Two more horse-drawn steamers were bought in 1896 and 1900. A few years later, in 1909, the first motorised fire engines arrived. The number of firemen again increased and by 1914 there were more than forty, with crews based at the Redland, St George and Bedminster police stations as well as at Bridewell Street. But there were many serious fires in the early years of the twentieth century and the brigade was frequently hard-pressed to contain them. Three firemen died at fires between 1906 and 1916.

The 1920s brought further improvements with more motor pumps, a motor turntable ladder and a new fireboat. Working hours were reduced in 1926 when the two-platoon system was introduced. Previously the firemen were continuously on duty with only one day off per week. Now they worked alternate weeks of day and night duties and did not have to live at, or close to, the fire station.

Bridewell Street Fire Station was completely rebuilt in the late 1920s and transformed into a thirteen-bay station with workshops, offices and living accommodation on upper floors for senior officers and their families. The Bedminster and St George Fire Stations were closed. Redland had closed in 1926 when its firemen and Dennis pump were transferred to a new station at Green Lane, Avonmouth.

The brigade tackled many serious fires in the early 1930s and the superintendent asked the Fire Brigade Committee for an increase in manpower. The situation was such that at times it was necessary to call in off-duty men to reinforce crews tackling major fires.

Gradually manning levels improved and by 1936 the brigade had one superintendent, two inspectors, seven sergeants and seventy-five constables. In that year it was necessary to reopen the St George station because of expansion of the eastern suburbs of the city and increased traffic congestion.

The worsening international situation in the late 1930s led to the Government setting up the Auxiliary Fire Service. Bristol Fire Brigade recruited almost 1,000 full-time auxiliary firemen and over 2,000 part-timers. Thirty-one auxiliary fire stations were opened. More than 200 extra fire pumps were acquired but the force proved woefully inadequate during the heavy air raids of the winter of 1940–1941 and reinforcements had to be called in from other areas to help. Twenty-three members of the fire service died tackling fires during the Blitz in Bristol. The Government set up the National Fire Service (NFS) on 18 August 1941 and Bristol Fire Brigade became part of Fire Force No.17 within Region 7. Bristol suffered no more major air raids but NFS units from the city went to Bath in April 1942 to help fight Blitz fires there.

The fire service was returned to local authority control on 1 April 1948. Bristol Fire Brigade was re-established, with 235 firemen operating from six stations, manning six pumps, five pump escapes, three turntable ladders, two fireboats and other appliances, but the brigade was no longer part of Bristol Constabulary. Just over 2,000 emergency calls were answered in the following year. More than 25 per cent were chimney fires. Two major incidents involving oil products occurred in 1951. An oil fire at Avonmouth was the largest of its type to date in peacetime. A garage explosion in the St Paul's district caused eleven deaths.

A six-year building programme to replace five of the city's fire stations started with the opening of a new one at Speedwell Road in December 1951, but financial restrictions slowed the programme and it took a further thirteen years to replace the other four. The appliance fleet was modernised with sixteen new first-line appliances between 1950 and 1963. Pre-war pumps with open bodies and wartime utility conversions were replaced by limousine-bodied vehicles equipped with radio.

The number of emergency calls rose almost every year during the 1960s. Increasingly the brigade was called out to non-fire incidents such as road traffic accidents. Extra equipment was carried on pumps to deal with these calls. A new rescue tender was purchased in 1967.

As working hours for firemen were reduced more men were recruited to compensate so that by 1974 more than 300 were employed. The brigade was now responding to more than 4,000 emergency calls annually, but the number of first-line appliances remained the same as it had been in 1948.

After years of frustration looking for a suitable site, a new headquarters and central fire station was opened in 1973 at Temple Back, and a ninety-five-year link with the old Bridewell Street site was broken. But Temple Back would remain the headquarters of Bristol Fire Brigade for little more than a year, as on 1 April 1974 the brigade lost its separate identity when it became part of the new County of Avon Fire Brigade. A new era of firefighting in Bristol had begun.

Dennis Hill
Keynsham
November 2006

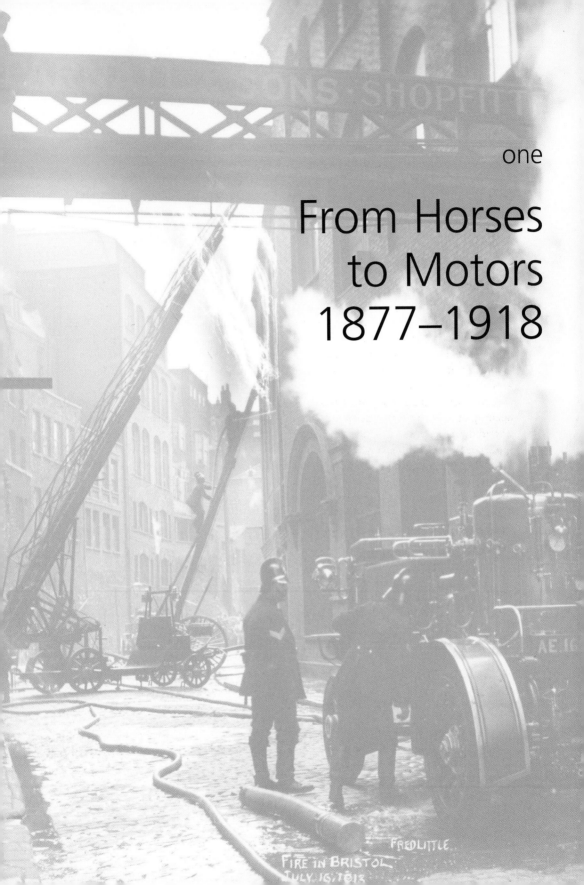

one

# From Horses to Motors 1877–1918

FRED LITTLE
FIRE IN BRISTOL
JULY 16, 1913

*Left:* Alfred Robert Tozer, first superintendent of Bristol Fire Brigade 1877–1879. After only two years in Bristol he was appointed Chief Officer of the much larger Birmingham Fire Brigade, a post he held with distinction for almost thirty years. He was described by a Birmingham MP in 1899 as 'the most accomplished fireman in the Kingdom'. (Author's Collection)

*Below:* Imperial Fire Office manual engine. One of six insurance companies that ran fire brigades in Bristol prior to 1877, Imperial retained this engine to attend out-of-town fires after all the other insurance companies passed their equipment to Bristol Corporation when Bristol Fire Brigade was set up. The Imperial brigade's superintendent, William Brown, was killed at a fire just outside the city boundary in 1891. The engine is now preserved at Bristol Industrial Museum. (Bristol Industrial Museum)

*Above:* The earliest known surviving photograph of Bristol Fire Brigade, taken in 1882, showing the Merryweather 360 gallons-per-minute (gpm) horse-drawn steam fire engine (steamer), delivered in 1877. In 1880 part of the police building at Bridewell was adapted to provide living quarters for the superintendent, dormitory accommodation for single men, a watch room, offices and additional stabling. (Author's Collection)

*Right:* There were many small, independent fire brigades in the Bristol area during late Victorian times. Often these were formed by businesses to protect their factories. Others looked after hospitals and similar institutions. This group of firemen is typical. They are standing in front of what appears to be a small hose cart. They could tackle small fires or perhaps even hold a more serious outbreak in check pending the arrival of the Bristol Fire Brigade. (Mrs Judith Cameron)

The firefighting capacity of Bristol Fire Brigade was increased substantially with the delivery of the fire float *Fire Queen* in January 1885. Many high-risk industrial premises lined the banks of the River Avon in central Bristol and the float could supply powerful jets to assist in extinguishing major fires. The float was built in London by Shand Mason, who also made horse-drawn steamers. (Avon Fire & Rescue Service)

*Fire Queen* was moored at Redcliffe. The uniform of Bristol Constabulary's river police, who provided the crew, had a distinctly nautical appearance with round caps, reefer jackets and sweaters. Here they pose with a range of land-based equipment including a steamer, a wheeled escape and a manual engine. John Thomas Gotts, who was appointed to head Bristol Fire Brigade in 1891, is at the right of the front row. (Mrs Valerie Glassenbury)

The wheeled escapes of the type pictured with the river police were hand-propelled to fires in the upright position. They weighed at least fifteen hundredweight and the men who pushed them often arrived at a fire too exhausted to carry out rescue work immediately. By the late 1890s the escapes were mounted on horse-drawn tenders. This one was based at Redland Police Station. (Avon Fire & Rescue Service)

At 2.15 a.m. on 1 September 1898 a fire was discovered in a four-storey clothing factory in Colston Street near the city centre. Flames, already through the roof when firemen arrived, soon spread to the adjoining Colston Hall, the city's premier public meeting venue. John Gotts stands with firemen in the ruins of the hall that was 'entirely gutted', according to the official report. (*Bristol Evening Post and Press*)

Extensions to the Bristol boundary in 1897 led to a doubling of the fire brigade's strength to twenty-eight men, excluding the river police. After a second Merryweather horse-drawn steamer named *Cabot* had been purchased in 1896, this third one, built by William Rose & Co. of Salford was delivered in 1900. But Rose, a former Chief Officer of Manchester Fire Brigade, could not compete with the London firms of Merryweather and Shand Mason. His company stopped building steamers in 1902, but continued to make other firefighting gear. (Roger Simpson)

The William Rose steamer was allocated to a new fire station adjoining St George police station in east Bristol. The local volunteer fire brigade was disbanded, as were those in four other districts swallowed up in the boundary extension, and altogether seventy part-time firemen were made redundant. By this time the population of Bristol exceeded 300,000, an increase of almost 50 per cent over that of 1877. (Reece Winstone Archive)

A horse-drawn chemical engine. This model was converted for Bristol Fire Brigade by Merryweather's from an old manual engine. In the top of the water tank was a small container of sulphuric acid. When the container was punctured the acid reacted with bicarbonate of soda that had been added to the water and produced carbon dioxide gas to force the water at high pressure through the hose reel. (Ian Scott Collection)

A drill with the chemical engine at Bridewell Street Fire Station. Bristol Waterworks Co. expressed fears that if the engine's tank was refilled with water direct from the mains, chemical residues in the tank might flow back into the mains and contaminate drinking water supplies. Somehow the problem was resolved and chemical engines remained in use in Bristol for almost twenty years. Motor-driven versions were introduced in 1909. (Ian Scott Collection)

By the early 1900s Bristol's city centre docks were less busy. Larger ships, unable to navigate the narrow channels of the tidal River Avon, used new docks downstream at Avonmouth, where the river joined the Severn Estuary. Several miles from the centre of Bristol, Avonmouth was beyond easy reach of Bristol Fire Brigade's horse-drawn appliances and in 1904 the Docks Committee commissioned this steam-powered fire float *Salamander* for use at Avonmouth Docks. (Bristol Industrial Museum)

This model of *Salamander* was made in 1938. The fire float itself remained in service for more than thirty years before being replaced in 1936. Built by G.K. Stothert & Co. of Hotwells, the float's crew was originally drawn from the river police but Bristol Fire Brigade took over these duties in 1931. (Fred Hooper)

A Saturday afternoon fire on 4 November 1905 badly damaged three substantial business premises in Colston Avenue, and a large crowd, including football fans returning from a match at Bristol City's ground, were there to watch. All three of Bristol Fire Brigade's steamers attended and eight jets were needed to extinguish the fire. The John Wright building would again be destroyed by fire during a German air raid in 1941 (see page 62). (Reece Winstone Archive)

One of the appliances attending the fire in Colston Avenue was the William Rose steamer from St George, here seen on the move in what appears to be a posed shot. It is easy to imagine the excitement that would have been aroused in the watching crowd as it arrived on the scene at the gallop. The horses would then have had to be unhitched and led away to a quieter spot while firefighting took place. (Avon Fire & Rescue Service)

Bristol Fire Brigade uniform of the early 1900s. The style would change little during the next forty years. The practice of showing the man's brigade number on the tunic breast was common. In the 1930s Bristol firemen had their numbers on the tunic collar and on the front of their helmets. (Avon Fire & Rescue Service)

THE FATAL FIRE
AT DERHAM LTD BOOT FACTORY
ST JAMES'S STREET,
BRISTOL.
DAMAGE £60.000.

'Bristol's Big Blaze' was at Derhams' seven-storey boot and shoe factory in Barton Street on 27 March 1906; it was described in the *Western Daily Press* as 'a fire that no water could touch'. Postcards of the fire were published and doubtless sold in large numbers, especially as, tragically, a fireman died when the front wall of the factory collapsed. (Ian Scott Collection)

*Right:* The fireman who died was Arthur Wale. He was the first member of Bristol Fire Brigade to lose his life on duty. The entry in Bristol Constabulary's occurrence book read, 'Fire at Derhams, 27-3-06. Attended by 29 firemen and 6 river police; 3 steamers, 1 chemical engine, 2 escapes, 5,000ft of hose used. Brigade in attendance 84 hours. Fireman Arthur Wale killed by front wall falling out. Sergeant Harrison seriously injured.' (Mrs Valerie Glassenbury)

*Below:* Arthur Wale had been based at Bedminster police station and here his coffin, borne on a fire tender, leaves the station for the funeral service at St Mary Redcliffe church. A local newspaper described him as 'a man of ripe experience whose long service in the Brigade had commanded the esteem of his officers and comrades.' He left a widow and eight children. Sergeant (later Inspector) Harrison would also die on duty, in a building collapse after a fire in Old Market Street on 2 August 1916. (Mrs Valerie Glassenbury)

*Left:* The top three floors of the Merchant Venturers' College in Unity Street were burnt out on 9 October 1906 in a night-time fire so bright that newspaper reports described it as being 'like a sunrise'. All available firemen were called in. Water was pumped from *Fire Queen*, moored at Broad Quay, to supplement jets from three steamers. The college was rebuilt and later became the city's College of Commerce. (Author's Collection)

*Below:* John Gotts, seated centre, and members of Bristol Fire Brigade who fought the Merchant Venturers' College fire. As a direct result of increases in brigade numbers since he took charge in 1891, John Gotts was promoted to Chief Inspector in 1898 and to Superintendent in 1906. Thus he was on a par with other superintendents in Bristol Constabulary. (Avon Fire & Rescue Service)

*Above:* The size of the brigade was increased again following the Merchant Venturers' College fire. There had been another major extension to the city boundary in 1904 and twice as many fires were now being attended annually than there were in 1877. New appliances were purchased, including this combined chemical engine and escape carrier, built by John Morris & Co. Ltd of Salford on a Belsize chassis. (John Thompson)

*Below:* The combination machine went to Bedminster Fire Station, while this similar model without an escape was allocated to Bridewell Street. John Morris sent drivers to Bristol to teach members of the brigade how to operate the new appliances. After extensive trials and a few modifications they entered service early in 1909. Petrol was supplied by Shell Petroleum at 10*d* per gallon. (Reece Winstone Archive)

Shand Mason self-propelled steamer registered AE 1623, also new in 1909. Its top speed was 20mph. It had a 500gpm pump and could throw a 1¾in jet to a height of 170ft. But it took several minutes to get the steamer up to full working pressure, and the model soon became obsolete as companies such as Merryweather, Dennis and Leyland developed improved petrol engine motor pumps. (Avon Fire & Rescue Service)

Bridewell Street Fire Station decorated for the Coronation of King George V, 22 June 1911. The front of the John Morris chemical engine can be seen. At this time firemen worked a continuous duty system, with one day's leave a week, and had to live at or near the fire station. Single men had dormitory accommodation at the station. Married men and their families occupied houses in nearby Silver Street. (Avon Fire & Rescue Service)

Bristol Fire Brigade's horse-drawn Magirus turntable ladder and Shand Mason self-propelled steamer at a fire at Messrs Morley & Sons, rag, rope and metal merchants, in Fairfax Street, 16 July 1913. The turntable ladder, supplied by John Morris in 1908, had a working height of 72ft. It did much good work during its years of service, but became obsolete as self-propelled motor versions were developed. (Fred Little Collection)

Fire at H.H. & S. Budgett, wholesale provision merchants, opposite Bristol Constabulary HQ, Bridewell Street, 9 August 1913. The Shand Mason steamer supplies four hose lines. Its suction is set into a canvas dam, fed from hose lines connected to hydrants. Forty firemen attended and as well as the Shand Mason, two steamers, two chemical engines and two escapes were deployed. (Fred Little Collection)

Superintendent Gotts with Dennis motor pump AE 4905, delivered in October 1914. It was named *The James Cann* after Bristol's Chief Constable. Some fire brigades regularly named fire engines after local dignitaries, but this is the only known instance in Bristol, apart from the fireboat named after Councillor Endres Gane. (Ian Scott Collection)

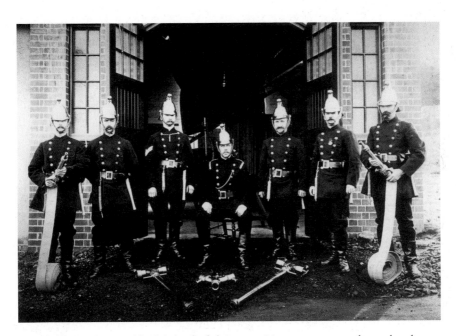

In communities just outside the city firefighting provisions were not as advanced as they were in Bristol. Brislington, on the south-east boundary, applied unsuccessfully in the 1890s for Bristol Fire Brigade to attend fires in its area, and had a small volunteer brigade equipped with little more than a hose cart. They are seen here outside their new station opened in Hollywood Road in 1912. (Brislington Conservation and History Society)

Dennis Brothers of Guildford supplied a second pump, AE 4906, to Bristol Fire Brigade in 1914 and also this general purpose van, AE 4907, on a similar chassis in 1915. In 1926 the van was converted into a motor pump and subsequently sold in 1930 to Portishead Fire Brigade where it remained in service into the Second World War. (Ian Scott Collection)

The strength of Bristol Fire Brigade was reduced considerably during the First World War as men were called up for military service. By February 1916 the brigade had only twenty-eight men instead of forty. Thirty-five special constables were enrolled to serve as auxiliary firemen. Some are seen here with Superintendent Gotts. (Avon Fire & Rescue Service)

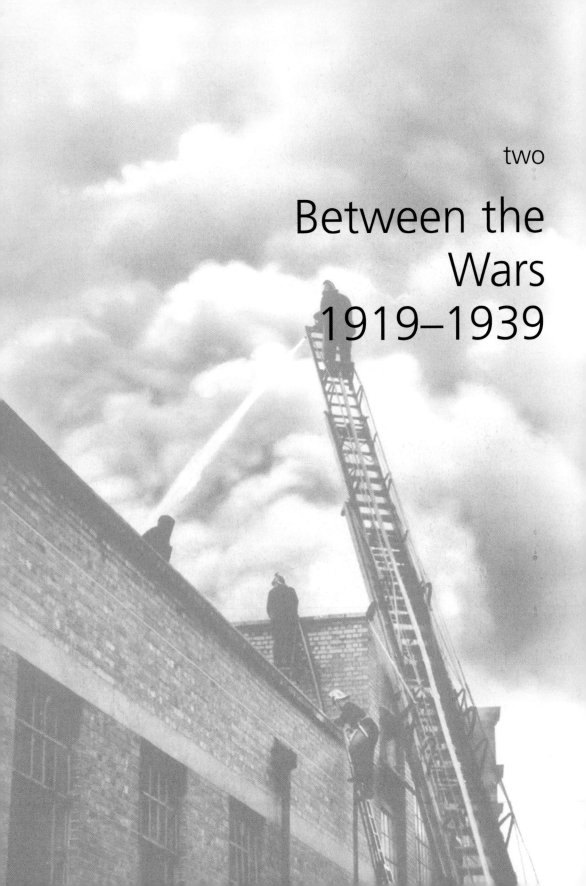

two

# Between the
# Wars
# 1919–1939

Superintendent Gotts retired in 1919 after twenty-eight years as Chief Officer and was succeeded by Fred Cade of Rotherham Fire Brigade, who immediately started modernising the brigade's equipment. These Leylands were delivered in 1921 to replace the Belsize/John Morris appliances and the Shand Mason steamer. (J. & D. Fisher)

Superintendent Cade (in cap) with members of the brigade on the new Leylands in Bridewell Street yard. The superintendent frequently rode to fires on the first turnout engine, with an inspector, sergeant and as many as six fire constables. The total strength of the brigade at this time was forty-five, at least twenty of whom were based at sub-stations around the city. (Avon Fire & Rescue Service)

Leyland tender HT 980. Although not equipped with a main pump, the tender frequently towed a trailer pump. The tender was also later adapted to carry foam equipment for tackling oil fires. (British Commercial Vehicle Museum Archive)

This Dennis trailer pump was an inexpensive yet valuable addition to Bristol Fire Brigade's equipment in the mid-1920s. It was often used at out-of-town fires where water sources such as ponds and streams might be inaccessible to full-size fire engines. (Avon Fire & Rescue Service)

Brislington Fire Brigade was motorised in the early 1920s with the purchase of a Ford lorry, but was disbanded when the area was fully absorbed into Bristol in 1933. The Hollywood Road station was used briefly by the AFS at the outbreak of the Second World War. In 2006 the building was still standing as part of a private house. (Brislington Conservation and History Society)

A few miles north of Brislington, the district of Kingswood had long been a centre of industry. Its fire brigade, short of money, went through difficult times in the early twentieth century and Bristol Fire Brigade was often called in to help. In 1926 the Kingswood brigade was disbanded following the firemen's protest at lack of equipment, but the problem was remedied when this new Merryweather pump was purchased. (Author's Collection)

Merryweather emergency car, registered HT 981, purchased in 1921. It carried lightweight rescue equipment including breathing apparatus. The car was replaced in 1930 by a converted Buick saloon CY 9454. It was larger and carried more equipment, including a ladder and hose reel. (Ian Scott Collection)

The Magirus horse-drawn turntable ladder was replaced by this Merryweather 90ft model registered HT 3528, based on an Aster chassis and delivered in September 1921. (Ian Scott Collection)

# 'THE "FIRST CALL" PUMP'

*The above picture illustrates three of the Leyland fire machines supplied to the Bristol Brigade.*

THE BRISTOL SUPERINTENDENT HAS PLACED THESE MACHINES IN THE DISTINCTIVE POSITION OF BEING THE "FIRST CALL" PUMPS.

*Leyland's hold the same position in most of the chief Fire Brigades of the Country.*

Leyland Motors of Leyland, Lancashire built their first motor fire engine in 1909. It went to Dublin Fire Brigade. By the end of the First World War the company was rivalling Dennis and Merryweather in supplying appliances to fire brigades throughout the British Isles. This advertisement in the March 1922 edition of *Fire* magazine capitalised on their recent deliveries to Bristol Fire Brigade. (Author's Collection).

Merryweather fireboat *Phoenix* was delivered to Bristol Fire Brigade in January 1921. The vessel came under its own power from the Merryweather works at Greenwich via the Kennet and Avon Canal. At Bath Superintendent Cade met the *Phoenix* and it is likely that Bristol firemen were on board during the last stage of its journey to Bristol. (Norman Tarling)

## Safoam "The Continuous Foam Stream System"

Another company using a sale to Bristol Fire Brigade to advertise its products was S. Dixon & Son Ltd of Swinegate, Leeds. They supplied foam-making equipment under the trade name 'Safoam'. Superintendent Cade stands with 'Safoam' cylinders. Each produced 150 gallons of firefighting foam. Four cylinders were carried on the Leyland tender. (John Terry)

*Above:* Shortly after 5 a.m. on 13 October 1928 a Leeds–Bristol passenger express train collided with a goods train in poor visibility at Charfield, Gloucestershire. The gas-lit carriages of the express caught fire and passengers were trapped. Bristol Fire Brigade, responding to a call 'Serious rail disaster. Send fire brigade at once', covered the sixteen and a half miles to Charfield in thirty-five minutes, despite dense fog. (Avon Fire & Rescue Service)

*Below:* Firemen from Stroud and Gloucester also attended, but it was too late to save fifteen of the passengers. An ambulance train staffed by St John Ambulance volunteers was sent from Bristol to carry the injured to the city's hospitals. Bristol Fire Brigade's trailer pump, using water drawn down from an overhead tank, supplied three jets used to prevent fire spreading to warehouses near the railway line. (Bob Vandereyt)

Water supplies for firefighting in some parts of central Bristol were improved in the late 1920s when Bristol Waterworks installed underground tanks fed by large diameter mains. Firemen drew water from the tanks using a suction hose, which was quicker than having to connect to several hydrants to obtain enough water at large fires. The first use of one of the tanks was at this fire on 28 April 1930 at A.W. Smith, Upholsterers, Portland Square. (Avon Fire & Rescue Service)

Bristol Fire Brigade purchased a second Merryweather turntable ladder, HY 331, in October 1930. It had the same working height, 90ft, as the previous one, but was based on an improved chassis with a Dorman six-cylinder engine of eighty brake horse power. It was also fitted with a 300gpm pump which could feed either a monitor at the head of the ladder or one fixed behind the driver's seat. (Avon Fire & Rescue Service)

Bristol Fire Brigade left Bridewell Street on 25 November 1927 and moved temporarily to a disused factory at Quakers Friars. The Bridewell Street building was demolished and a new thirteen-bay fire station with offices, workshops and living accommodation was built on the site. Here passers-by peer through the windows of the Bridewell Street frontage prior to the official opening on 5 November 1930. (Fred Hooper)

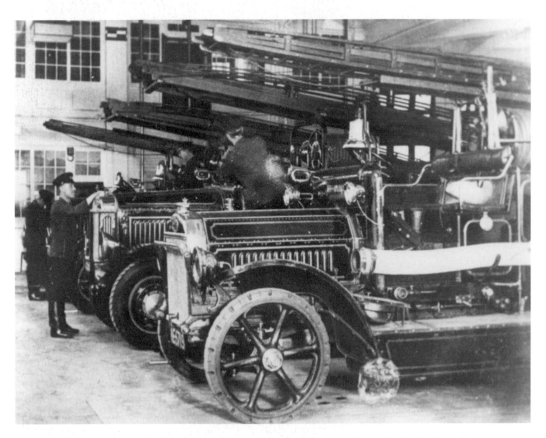

The seven bays opening onto Bridewell Street housed the superintendent's car, the Leyland tender, two pump escapes, a pump and two turntable ladders. Firemen polish the brass-work. The nine-year-old Leylands have now been fitted with pneumatic tyres, but the 1917 Dennis, nearest the camera, is still running on solid tyres. These made it prone to skidding, especially on wet cobblestone streets with tramlines. Pneumatic tyres were fitted to the Dennis in 1931. (Avon Fire & Rescue Service)

Merryweather turntable ladder HY 331 in use at a night-time fire. A fireman at the head of the ladder directs the monitor but it could also be controlled from ground level. This fire is typical of many that occurred in central Bristol in the 1930s, in terraces of old houses that had been converted to commercial use for the manufacture of furniture, cardboard and paper products, all of which carried a high fire risk. (Bob Vandereyt)

Leyland Motors introduced new models in the early 1930s. HY 1801, based on a Lioness chassis, was delivered to Bristol Fire Brigade on 16 May 1931. Note the mid-ships pump, unusual windscreen and white wall pneumatic tyres. The appliance was fitted with electric starting, but two days after its delivery Sergeant Marsh fractured an arm starting the engine with the starting handle. (British Commercial Vehicle Museum Archive)

Fire Constable James Sanders died from natural causes on 3 June 1931. His colleagues are seen here parading for his funeral. As with all sergeants and constables in Bristol Constabulary the men's division letters and numbers are shown on their helmets and tunic collars. The fire brigade was G Division and James Sanders' number, 31, was shown on the helmet-shaped floral tribute carried by the fireman on the right. (Fred Hooper)

Leyland HY 1801 at a fire on 26 October 1931 at the English Corrugating Paper Co. Ltd, Portland Square, alongside Merryweather turntable ladder HY 331. A film of this fire has survived and is preserved by Hampshire Library Service. In 1999, sixty-eight years after the fire, HY 1801 was driven by its owner David Berry to Portland Square for a meeting with a director of the English Corrugating Paper Co., then still trading in the square. The occasion was filmed for a television news programme. (Avon Fire & Rescue Service)

*Right:* Dennis pump AE 4905 went off the road on 15 March 1932, responding from Avonmouth Fire Station to a fire in the Lawrence Weston area. A newspaper reported, 'The firemen were undismayed at this mishap and ran the last part of the way to the fire'. The engine was repaired, sold for £75 in 1933 to Radstock Fire Brigade and was still operational at the start of the Second World War. (Fred Hooper)

*Below:* The other 1914 Dennis pump AE 4906 was taken by Leyland Motors in 1932 in part exchange against a new appliance HY 4979, seen here on the left alongside three other Leylands outside Bridewell Fire Station, 12 August 1932. The new Leyland cost £1,650, less £100 allowed for the part-exchanged Dennis. (British Commercial Vehicle Museum Archive)

Firemen demonstrate the use of a Merryweather jumping sheet. Bristol Fire Brigade appliances carried such sheets in the 1930s but there is no record of them ever being used in the city to rescue people from fires. (John Terry)

By 1932 the strength of Bristol Fire Brigade had increased to seventy-one. While constables were on the two-platoon system, sergeants and higher ranks remained on the old continuous duty system, living with their families in flats at headquarters. In July 1932 the brigade lined up to mark the retirement of Superintendent Cade, eighth from the left in the front row, next to Chief Constable Charles Maby, in the suit. (Avon Fire & Rescue Service)

Although the Leylands bought in the early 1930s were technically more advanced than earlier models, they still offered no protection for the crew in the event of an accident. On 11 June 1934 while responding from Bridewell Street to a fire at Avonmouth, HY 4979 collided with a car, skidded and overturned. Nine men were on the Leyland and one of them, Inspector John Crossman, was fatally injured. (Avon Fire & Rescue Service)

Inspector Crossman was given a brigade funeral with full honours, and 400 members of Bristol Constabulary paraded in uniform to pay their respects. John Crossman's widow and two small children had to vacate the married quarters at Bridewell Street after his successor, Joseph Young Kirkup, a sergeant in the Newcastle upon Tyne Police Fire Brigade, had been appointed. (*Bristol Evening Post and Press*)

Two weeks after Inspector Crossman's death the brigade's resources were severely stretched at a lunch-time fire on 26 June 1934 in the congested Milk Street area. The *Evening Post* reported, 'All available firemen were called to the scene and every appliance from the Central Fire Station employed.' The fire started in Epsteins, picture frame makers, and spread to five other buildings before being extinguished. (Avon Fire & Rescue Service)

During the Epsteins fire, people living nearby had to evacuate their homes and remove their furniture. Several houses were rendered uninhabitable and the occupants were accommodated in the nearby YMCA building. A relief fund was launched to help them re-establish their homes. (Fred Hooper)

*Right:* Francis Winteringham of Swansea Fire Brigade succeeded Fred Cade as Superintendent of Bristol Fire Brigade. He was riding with Inspector Crossman on HY 4979 at the time of the accident on 11 June 1934 but escaped injury, and was in charge of fighting the Epsteins fire. He carried on Fred Cade's campaign for an increase in brigade numbers, and eventually the Watch Committee agreed to recruit more firemen. By 1936 the strength of the brigade had increased to eighty-five. (*Bristol Evening Post and Press*)

*Below:* Leyland pump HY 9756, purchased in July 1933, featured in a booklet published in 1936 to mark the centenary of Bristol Constabulary. The booklet recorded that a Bristol Waterworks employee, described as a turncock, was on duty at Bridewell Street fire station every night. He rode to fires and made sure that enough water was available from the mains for firefighting. The arrangement was first set up in 1877, in response to the serious fires of 1876. (Author's Collection)

*Left:* Two turntable ladders in use at a night-time fire that badly damaged Bristol Assize Courts, 1 February 1935. Newspapers reported, 'Another disastrous West Country fire', but crews from Bridewell Street Fire Station prevented the outbreak spreading to adjoining buildings, and had it under control within two hours. (Avon Fire & Rescue Service)

*Below:* During the 1930s the Leyland motor tender and pumps carried sets of self-contained oxygen breathing apparatus (BA) of either half-hour or one hour duration, but no more than two sets were carried on each appliance. Siebe Gorman 'Proto' sets are being tested at Bridewell Street Fire Station. Sets of this pattern would continue in use until the 1960s when they were replaced by compressed air sets. (*Bristol Evening Post and Press*)

The 1921 turntable ladder HT 3528 collapsed at a fire in Fairfax Street on 6 July 1935, but the fireman on it suffered only minor injuries after falling through the roof of Coombs & Co.'s building. A St John ambulance in attendance was used as a canteen van to supply refreshments to firemen during the protracted incident. Volunteers from either St John or the City and Marine Ambulance Corps attended every fire call in Bristol during the 1920s and 1930s, a fee of up to £1 per call being paid by the Watch Committee for this service. (Avon Fire & Rescue Service)

An independent assessor examined the damaged turntable ladder afterwards but no cause for the collapse could be determined. Merryweather's were satisfied that the appliance was being operated properly at the fire. The company supplied this model with 100ft steel ladders as a replacement in February 1936. Registered as CAE 965, it cost £3,510, minus an allowance of £225 for the old machine. (John Terry)

Also delivered in 1936 was this Leyland Cub pump CHW 353. It was allocated to Avonmouth Fire Station. The Leyland's narrow wheelbase made it ideal for negotiating the minor roads and lanes around the rural parts of the station's turnout area. It would remain in service for twenty-six years. (British Commercial Vehicle Museum Archive)

Another Dennis in trouble! The 1917 model AE 6719, now fitted with pneumatic tyres and again operating from Avonmouth Fire Station, is being recovered from a ditch by means of a chain hoist. When the Watch Committee authorised its replacement in 1937, it was retained as a reserve machine, in view of the perceived need for extra fire pumps, should the country find itself at war. (Avon Fire & Rescue Service)

Avonmouth Fire Station, Green Lane. Cottages were also built in Green Lane for some of the firemen and their families. These firemen, while on duty, were allowed home for meals and were known as 'homers', while colleagues who lived further away and had meals at the station were referred to as 'towners'. (Avon Fire & Rescue Service)

Chevrolet tender HY 2485, with bodywork by W. Moore & Sons of Monmouth Street, Bath, purchased by Bristol Docks Committee and delivered on 1 May 1931. It was crewed by Bristol Fire Brigade and kept at Avonmouth Fire Station but could only be used to attend fires at Avonmouth Docks. Note the 'Safoam' cylinders on the rear platform (see page 33). (Bristol Record Office)

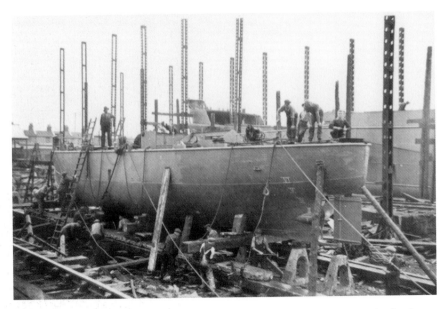

In 1931 the Docks Committee also undertook responsibility for maintaining the fire float *Salamander*, and Bristol Fire Brigade agreed to crew it. In 1936 *Salamander* was replaced by *Endres Gane*, here seen under construction in the Bristol yard of Charles Hill & Sons Ltd, and named after a member of the fire brigade committee. Each vessel gave thirty-one years' service, spanning more than six decades from 1905 to 1967. (Mike Williams)

The crew of *Endres Gane* in 1936. From left to right: H. Webber, H. Maynell, Sgt H. Humphrys, R. Cook and J. Gore. They were based at Avonmouth Fire Station, which had a staff of one sergeant and fourteen firemen. Even when there was a large fire elsewhere in Bristol, Avonmouth firemen were seldom called to assist. Their priority was to be available for fires in the Avonmouth area, particularly in the docks. (Fred Hooper)

*Right:* An early morning fire at Russells Builders Merchants on 7 August 1937 led to the evacuation of seventy-one occupants from the nearby YMCA. Bristol Fire Brigade attended with three pumps, two turntable ladders and a fireboat. A water curtain was put up to protect Colston Hall and the fire was confined to Russells building. Newspapers praised the firemen's 'finest qualities in handling a difficult and dangerous situation'. (Ian Scott Collection)

*Below:* The fireboat at the Russells fire was *Phoenix II*, built in Bristol by Charles Hill & Sons Ltd in 1934 to replace the original *Phoenix*. But *Phoenix II* was renamed *Pyronaut* in 1938 when it was found that another vessel named *Phoenix* was already registered at Lloyds. *Pyronaut*, based at Redcliffe, remained in service until 1973. (Avon Fire & Rescue Service)

Another serious fire in the high-risk St Paul's district, 7 September 1938. It started in Thos. Williams & Son (Bristol) Ltd timber works in Cave Street and Portland Square. Four buildings were burnt out in a fire to which 'practically all the resources of the Bristol Fire Brigade were mobilised' according to the *Evening Post*. The turntable ladder CAE 965 was damaged by a collapsing wall and two firemen were slightly injured. (Avon Fire & Rescue Service)

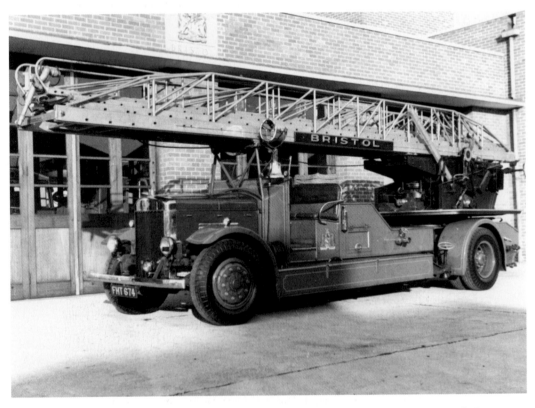

The damaged turntable ladder was returned to Merryweather's for repair and the company was asked to urgently deliver a new turntable ladder already on order. This was done and the new appliance arrived in Bristol on 5 October 1938. It cost £3,998 and was registered as FHT 674. It remained in service until 1965 and is seen here at Speedwell Fire Station during the 1950s. (Avon Fire & Rescue Service)

*Above left and right:* Until 1938 Bristol firemen wore black leather helmets with combs and edges of brass, as seen here. They were replaced in March 1938 by a lighter model made of cork, once again in black. It was topped with a large comb, and had a wider skirt to give more protection to the neck and ears. (Avon Fire & Rescue Service)

The letters BPFB – Bristol Police Fire Brigade – appeared on the front of the new helmet, surrounded by a laurel wreath. Hollywood film star Tom Mix, visiting Bristol, tries one for size, assisted by Superintendent Albert Maunder. The helmets remained in use for only three years and when the NFS was set up in August 1941 all firemen were issued with grey steel helmets. Before this regular firemen in Bristol Fire Brigade wore red steel helmets to attend Blitz fires. (Avon Fire & Rescue Service)

In March 1937, in response to a Home Office memorandum on emergency fire brigade organisation, Chief Constable Charles Maby started to advertise for recruits to join the Bristol Auxiliary Fire Service (AFS). It was calculated that 1,132 full-time and 2,632 part-time firemen were needed. Women were to be employed for communications, clerical and canteen duties. These AFS recruits are seen in east Bristol with the Leyland pump escape based at St George Fire Station. (Fred Hooper)

It was feared that gas would be used in air attacks and some AFS men were issued with special gas-proof suits, as seen here. The suits must have been unbearably hot to wear for any length of time. Elsewhere, other AFS men lacked even basic firefighting uniforms and had little more than the overalls, caps and boots seen in the previous photograph, almost up to the time of the first air raids. (Fred Hooper)

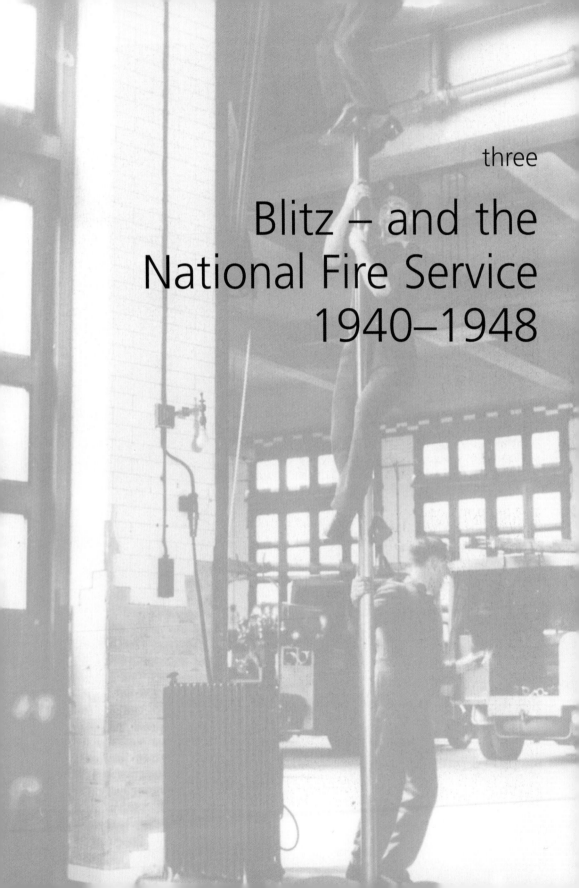

# three

# Blitz – and the National Fire Service 1940–1948

AFS recruits gained experience attending fires with the regular brigade. Here they are seen on the right, wearing steel helmets, at a fire in Farr's Lane, Prince Street, January 1940. A few months later they would face the horrors of Blitz fires that brought death and destruction to the city. (Ian Scott Collection)

*Right:* This page from the first edition of the Bristol AFS magazine *The Jet*, published in January 1940, shows the brigade's senior officers. Chief Inspector Kirkup was responsible for running the city's AFS. He had eighteen years' firefighting experience, but the four recently recruited divisional officers had virtually none. Training the AFS put a huge burden on members of the regular brigade. (Monty Britton)

*Below:* Among the AFS volunteers was Fred Hooper. This certificate shows him to be a trained messenger. The lower age limit for messengers was sixteen but proof of age was not required. Fred joined before his fifteenth birthday and saw plenty of action during the Blitz through 1940–1941. Later he became an NFS fireman and subsequently served in Bristol Fire Brigade. (Fred Hooper)

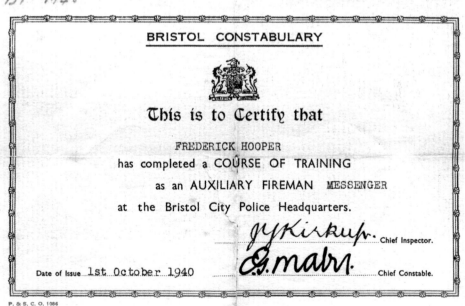

AFS firemen train with a self-propelled pump in the Fishponds area of Bristol. These pumps, issued by the Home Office, carried up to eight men, most standing alongside the ladder, but there was no water on board. During air raids this often meant the difference between saving and losing a burning building, as water mains were frequently damaged by bombs. (Fred Pincott)

Attempts to overcome water shortages included the provision of mobile dam units that could be filled from an open water supply and then driven to the fire. This example was based on a second-hand Bristol 'B' type single-deck bus, new to the Bristol Tramways & Carriage Co. Ltd's fleet in 1928, and built at the company's Brislington works. (Fred Pincott)

Many of Bristol's AFS stations were in requisitioned premises, including commercial garages, factories and schools. There was also one at Bristol General Hospital. The hospital had been built in Victorian times with units on the ground floor that could be let, with the rents used to help finance hospital running costs. One unit became an AFS station and here the crew are seen outside. (Fred Hooper)

The Home Office subsidised the cost of a number of turntable ladders for wartime emergency firefighting. This Leyland/Merryweather GHW 415 was delivered to Bristol three days before the devastating air raid of 24 November 1940. It has a masked headlight and white-edged mudguards to comply with blackout regulations. The bodywork is painted in AFS grey, apart from the engine cover, made of special steel and unpainted. (British Commercial Vehicle Museum Archive)

The first air raid on Bristol was on 25 June 1940 when casualties were few, but on Sunday 24 November 1940 the centre of the city was devastated, with hundreds of fires caused by incendiary bombs. Bristol Fire Brigade and AFS did what they could, but there were too many fires and not enough firemen. Eighty-one other brigades sent reinforcements, but the worst damage had been done before most of them arrived. This is Broadmead, near Bridewell Street Fire Station the following morning. (The Facey Collection at Bristol Record Office)

Park Street on the morning of 25 November 1940, with one third of the street's buildings destroyed. During the raid there were severe water shortages due to huge demands on the mains and damage to some of them caused by high explosive bombs. At least 200 people, including eight firemen, died in the raid. (The Facey Collection at Bristol Record Office)

Among the eighty-one brigades that sent help to Bristol on the night of 24 November 1940 was that of the Chipping Sodbury Rural District Council, whose boundary met Bristol's at Filton. This tender for their Filton AFS section is being 'christened' during winter weather with snow on the ground. (Avon Fire & Rescue Service)

The tender is much more typical of the appliances used by AFS crews than the self-propelled unit shown on page 56. Most of the pumps issued by the Home Office were trailers, as seen here, and local authorities had to purchase second-hand vehicles to tow them. Often such vehicles were in poor condition and proved to be mechanically unreliable. Another photograph of the tender seen here shows its front tyres to be completely bald! (Avon Fire & Rescue Service)

Fire crews tackling Blitz fires often worked for hours on end without refreshments. There were just a few canteen vans, such as this one, from which Mrs Winifred Tribe is serving tea. Mrs Tribe and her AFS firewomen colleagues bravely took their vans out to firemen at the height of the air raids. (Avon Fire & Rescue Service)

Their Majesties King George VI and Queen Elizabeth visited Bristol early in December 1940 to see the Blitz damage and meet members of the emergency services. Mrs Tribe is presented to Queen Elizabeth, with Chief Inspector Kirkup looking on. Mrs Tribe was later awarded the MBE for her work during the Blitz, not only in Bristol but also in Portsmouth and Plymouth. (Avon Fire & Rescue Service)

*Right:* After further serious raids on Bristol in December with hundreds more casualties, there was another on the night of 3–4 January 1941. Sub-zero temperatures made the firemen's task even more difficult, as water from hoses froze. A turntable ladder at the General Hospital could not be moved for three days. Its ladders were frozen in the elevated position and firemen had to chip the ice off with axes. (The Facey Collection at Bristol Record Office)

*Below:* Not far from the General Hospital a large granary at Princes Wharf, Wapping Road, was destroyed and again the effect of ice can be seen. Some reinforcing crews in Bristol that night came from Devon, travelling seventy miles on open fire engines in blackout conditions. They included Exeter Fire Brigade's turntable ladder and a Leyland Cub pump from Budleigh Salterton. (The Facey Collection at Bristol Record Office)

The last major air attack on Bristol took place in April 1941, just before Easter, and became known as the Good Friday raid. It was considered the worst since 24 November 1940. This fire destroyed John Wright's premises in Colston Avenue (see page 17). The fire was caused by an oil bomb that killed four AFS men. Bath Fire Brigade's Merryweather turntable ladder GL 4110 is at work. (The Facey Collection at Bristol Record Office)

Leyland pump escape HHT 183, delivered in 1941, was the first Bristol Fire Brigade appliance to have an enclosed crew cab, and the last purchased by the brigade before nationalisation. The rear doors of the cab have been removed but were refitted several years later. It usually ran as first pump at Bridewell Street, carrying ladders instead of a wheeled escape. (Avon Fire & Rescue Service)

It was the countrywide organisational problems experienced in tackling Blitz fires in the winter of 1940–1941 that led to the Government nationalising the fire service. This map shows Bristol and the surrounding areas that made up Fire Force No.17 as originally established on 18 August 1941 and changes made subsequently. (Fred Hooper)

By the time the NFS was established, German air raids on England had virtually ceased, as the bulk of the Luftwaffe was transferred to the Eastern Front. But in Bristol on 28 August 1942 in Broad Weir, a single aircraft dropped a 500lb bomb that exploded on impact. Burning petrol from a car that was hit set fire to three double-deck buses loaded with passengers, mostly women and children. (Reece Winstone Archive)

Emergency vehicles responding to the incident were delayed by heavy traffic and the chaos after the attack. By the time a route had been cleared it was too late to save many of those who had been trapped in the burning buses. Forty-five died. It was the highest death toll for any single Blitz incident in Bristol. (*Bristol Evening Post and Press*)

One of the largest NFS stations in Bristol was in Coronation Road, near Bedminster Bridge and just across the river from Bristol General Hospital. A garage block belonging to the Imperial Tobacco Co. had been taken over and temporary buildings were added to provide accommodation for personnel. One of the NFS watches is seen alongside a Leyland Beaver/Merryweather turntable ladder GXA 74, new in 1943. (Trevor Palfrey)

After a short time in Bristol, GXA 74 was moved by the NFS to Cheltenham. Here it continued in service with Gloucestershire Fire Service after 1 April 1948. Withdrawn from service in 1964, it was later used by a company for maintenance work on high buildings. It is seen here during that period, in Wine Street, Bristol. (Ron Henderson)

When women were first recruited into the AFS their duties were somewhat limited. One of their main roles was in communications. Later, as members of the NFS, some went from Bristol to Bath to assist with communications work following the air raids on the city in April 1942. This group is clearly dressed for travel, wearing greatcoats and carrying steel helmets and respirators. (Betty Peet)

Gradually women took on other duties, including hose repairs. The hose seen here is a cotton-jacketed rubber type from the United States of America. Large quantities were imported to make up for shortages in home-produced unlined linen hose. The bulkier American hose took up more locker space on appliances, so fewer lengths could be carried. (Fred Pincott)

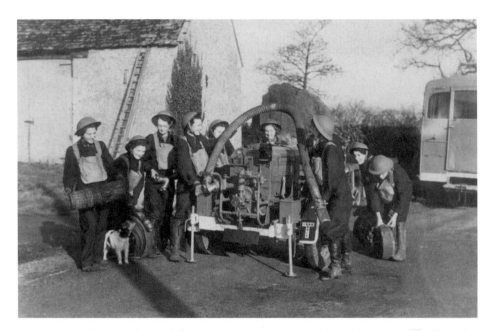

Some women also trained in firefighting. Here a group get to work with a trailer pump, although there is no evidence of them being involved in tackling Blitz fires. But their bravery could not be disputed, especially those who delivered petrol and refreshments to firemen during the night-time air raids on Bristol. (Avon Fire & Rescue Service)

This canteen van at Stoke Hill Fire Station was converted from a commercial vehicle. The costs of doing so were paid for by the Bristol Girl Guides organisation. It appears to be the one in use by NFS women in the photograph on page 66. (Avon Fire & Rescue Service)

*Above:* In 1941 the wooden ladders on Merryweather turntable ladder HY 331 were said to be inoperable because of warping. Merryweather's fitted a set of steel ladders and the appliance is seen subsequently at NFS station 17-A-6 on Waters Road, Two Mile Hill, in east Bristol. The premises were a requisitioned mineral water factory. (Avon Fire & Rescue Service)

*Left:* Polishing the brass! In common with most fire appliances built before the Second World War, Merryweather turntable ladder HY 331 had brass fittings that required frequent cleaning. Despite its new steel ladders HY 331 was scrapped by the NFS a few years later. (Fred Pincott)

*Above:* Many second-hand vehicles were pressed into service to meet the demands of emergency wartime firefighting. This primitive foam tender based on a second-hand lorry was typical of adaptations made by NFS personnel. Later in the war, as better materials became available, NFS workshops were producing fire appliances with limousine bodywork. (Avon Fire & Rescue Service)

*Right:* Despite improvements in NFS appliances there was still one vital element missing: none of them were equipped with radio. Motorcyclists filled the communications gap. One always followed the first pump turning out from Bridewell Street Fire Station, ready to take back urgent messages for reinforcements if necessary. This NFS woman motorcyclist has goggles but does not wear a helmet. (Fred Pincott)

As the war progressed the NFS became increasing involved in the training of Fire Guards, who were organised into patrols near their homes or places of work in order to carry out first-aid-type firefighting. Thus fires could be kept in check, if not actually extinguished, before NFS crews reached the scene. Here NFS men from Bridewell Street Fire Station, with a trailer pump, drill with a team of Fire Guards. (Fred Hooper)

The NFS had enough tradesmen within its ranks to build complete fire stations, using hired plant and machinery. The men remained on call for fires, with their appliances parked near the building site ready for immediate turnout. Here a fire station appliance room is under construction. (Fred Hooper)

The Canadian Government sent a contingent of firemen to England in the aftermath of the Blitz in 1940–1941. One detachment of about sixty men came to Bristol in the autumn of 1942 and stayed for two years. They were based at an NFS-built fire station in the grounds of Clifton Theological College, Stoke Hill in the north-west of the city. Here some of them visit Blitz-damaged buildings. (Fred Hooper)

The Canadians settled in well and worked alongside other NFS units in Bristol. This Canadian crew won trophies competing in drills against NFS crews in the area in 1943. One of the serious fires they attended was that which broke out on the United States vessel *Pan Massachusetts* at Avonmouth Docks on 25 May 1944. (Fred Hooper)

UNION STRENGTHENS

*Above:* A special badge was designed to mark the co-operation between the Canadians and the NFS in Bristol. After the Canadians returned home towards the end of 1944, the station at Stoke Hill was occupied by the NFS. It later became Station 2 of Bristol Fire Brigade, and was eventually vacated in March 1959 when the lease on the land expired. A replacement station opened at Southmead Road, Westbury-on-Trym a year later. (Fred Hooper)

*Left:* Geoff Bennett served with the AFS and NFS in Bristol. He started a local fund in 1941 to assist the families of fire service colleagues who had died on duty. The fund merged with others around the country in 1943 to form the National Fire Service Benevolent Fund. More than sixty years later the fund, renamed the Fire Services National Benevolent Fund, still helps firefighters and their families in times of need. (Betty Peet)

Avonmouth Docks became a vital link during the build-up to the D-Day invasion on 6 June 1944. A great deal of material, much of it highly flammable, was handled and the NFS often stood by while cargoes were unloaded. Even so, things occasionally went wrong, as happened on 25 May 1944, when there was an explosion on board the US vessel *Pan Massachusetts*. (Fred Hooper)

The 11,015 ton vessel was carrying a cargo of petrol and ammunition, and after a second explosion a serious fire broke out amidships. NFS reinforcements arrived quickly and a concentrated foam attack was made on the main fire. Altogether 100 firefighters worked for eight hours to bring the outbreak under control. Jets were also supplied from two fireboats. Only 10 per cent of the petrol was lost but three members of the ship's crew died in the initial explosion. (Fred Hooper)

One of the fireboats at the *Pan Massachusetts* fire was *Endres Gane*. The other was one of the second-hand vessels purchased and adapted for emergency wartime firefighting. By 1944 the NFS had a total of 330 fireboats and barges in England, Scotland and Wales. Among these were *Denny*, *Diana* and *Irma Alice*, all based at or near Avonmouth. This is *Irma Alice*. (Fred Hooper)

United States military personnel attended firefighting courses in Bristol towards the end of the Second World War. Here some are seen thanking their NFS hosts at Bridewell Street Fire Station. (Betty Peet)

Bristol's Colston Hall, having survived the Blitz, succumbed to an early morning fire on 5 February 1945. It may have been caused by a discarded cigarette after a concert on the previous evening. NFS crews arrived within two minutes of the alarm being raised, but flames were already through the roof. One hundred firefighters with sixteen pumps and four turntable ladders used seventeen jets to fight the fire, but they were unable to save the building. (*Bristol Evening Post and Press*)

War in Europe came to an end in May 1945, and there were celebrations throughout the country. NFS personnel at Bridewell Street Fire Station joined in and Leyland pump DHY 496, festooned with revellers, was driven around the centre of Bristol. (Fred Hooper)

*Left:* Bridewell Street Fire Station, like many others in the 1930s, had sliding poles for firemen to reach the appliance room quickly from upper floors when an alarm was received. It was also not unknown for the children of fire officers living in quarters at the station to use them! But there was always the risk of an accident, and in June 1944 a fireman at Bridewell Street suffered fatal injuries when he fell 25ft from the sliding pole when responding to a fire call. (Fred Hooper)

*Below:* Apart from the sliding pole, another hazard was getting into bulky fire kit on a moving appliance. Leyland pump escape HY 4979 is about to leave Bridewell Street Fire Station. The Leyland has an unpainted steel engine cover that looked blue and was kept clean with an oily rag. Paint on engine covers could blister when the pump was operated for long periods at fires. (Betty Peet)

The pump escape emerges from the appliance room alongside Leyland pump HHT 183 showing NFS sign and station No.17-A-1 on the cab door. HY 4979 carries a Merryweather 50ft steel escape. A fireman stops passing traffic with a red flag. The flag system remained in use until the early 1970s. Hand lamps were used at night. (Betty Peet)

The use of Leyland HHT 183 as a pump escape seems to have been short-lived. This photograph, showing it carrying an 'Ajax' ladder, was probably taken at the same time as the one on page 62. The appliance usually operated as first pump at Bridewell Street Fire Station, as seen here. It was the tenth Leyland purchased by Bristol Fire Brigade. All gave more than twenty years' service. (Avon Fire & Rescue Service)

*Left:* The NFS continued for almost three years after the end of the Second World War, but eventually the Government returned fire brigades to local control by passing the Fire Services Act in 1947, and on 1 April 1948 Bristol Fire Brigade became one of 141 new fire brigades, all of which took responsibility for either a county or county borough, covering England and Wales. On the previous day a dramatic rescue had taken place in the Avon Gorge. (Richard Tazewell)

*Below:* Leading Fireman Tazewell (left) climbed onto the rock face from the top of a fully extended turntable ladder and brought to safety an eleven-year-old boy, stranded 100ft up on the side of the gorge. Next to L/F Tazewell is Fred Revelle GM, who became Deputy Chief Fire Officer of Bristol Fire Brigade in 1951, and Chief Fire Officer in 1967. (Richard Tazewell)

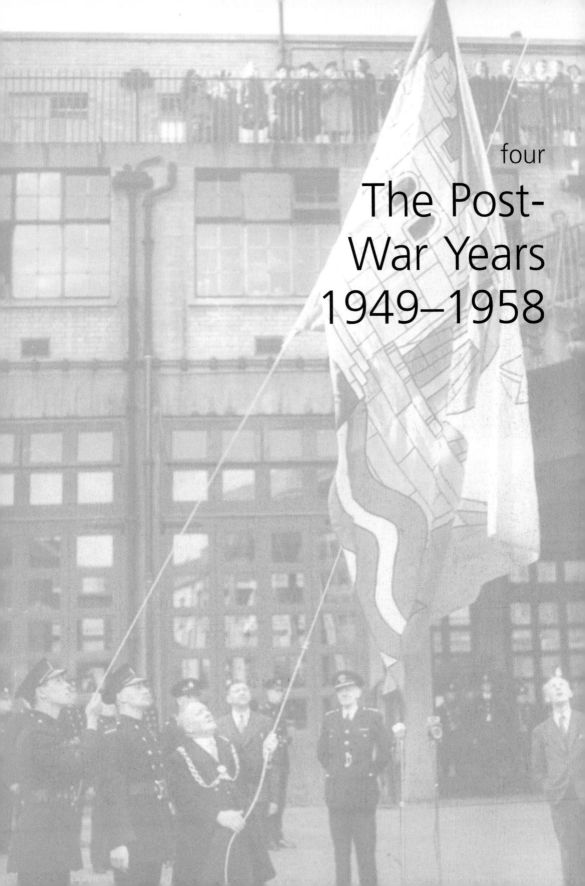

four

# The Post-War Years 1949–1958

*Left:* The Bristol flag is raised at Bridewell Street Fire Station at a ceremony on 1 April 1948 to mark the return of the fire service to local authority control. Joseph Young Kirkup (centre), who had been a Chief Inspector in the pre-war Bristol Fire Brigade and later on was Fire Force Commander of Fire Force No.17 in the NFS, was appointed Chief Fire Officer of the new brigade. (Fred Hooper)

*Below:* The Fire Services Act of 1947 abolished police fire brigades. Bristol Fire Brigade, no longer part of Bristol Constabulary, was now administered by a separate committee of Bristol City Council, instead of by a sub-committee of the Watch Committee. Another change from the pre-war regime was in the employment of women as members of the control room staff. Betty Peet (left) and Iris Hartree are on duty in the control room at Bridewell Street. (Betty Peet)

Bristol Fire Brigade assumed responsibility for running the city's ambulance service on 1 July 1948 and ambulances were kept at all six of the city's fire stations except Avonmouth. This impressive line up at Station 2, Stoke Hill, shows part of the total fleet of thirty-one ambulances and fifteen sitting-case cars. The station's normal complement was seven ambulances and two cars. (Fred Hooper)

Although some men were allocated solely to ambulance duties, operational firemen could be switched to emergency ambulance work at times of high demand. CFO Kirkup, in uniform, is at Station 2, accepting keys to new ambulances. On 1 April 1952 the running of Bristol's ambulance service passed to the city's Public Health Department and ambulances were kept at some Bristol Fire Stations for several years afterwards. (Fred Hooper)

When Bristol Fire Brigade was re-established on 1 April 1948, with none of its major appliances equipped with two-way radio, wireless cars provided a vital communications link between crews at a fire and the brigade's control room. At first ex-NFS military-style Ford estate cars were used, but these were replaced by Humber cars, such as this Super Snipe NHU 910, and Land Rovers. (Avon Fire & Rescue Service)

The Leyland pump HHT 183 is seen here after a major refit by brigade workshops in 1950. It was stripped to its chassis, the pump mechanism was overhauled, bodywork panels were renewed and the whole vehicle was re-sprayed. All brass fittings were chromium plated. It now carries roof-mounted 'FIRE' sign and siren, and is fitted with two-way radio. (Avon Fire & Rescue Service)

Also in 1950 a new Dennis F7 pump escape MHW 800, costing £3,400, was allocated to Station 1, Bridewell Street. It was equipped with a 900gpm mid-ships mounted pump and carried a 50ft Merryweather steel escape ladder. Powered by a Rolls-Royce B.80 Mk.10 petrol engine, it could accelerate from 0 to 60mph in forty-five seconds. (Avon Fire & Rescue Service)

Dennis/Merryweather 100ft turntable ladder GLW 424, delivered to the NFS in Bristol in 1942 and transferred to Bristol Fire Brigade on 1 April 1948. The Humber wireless car, the Leyland pump, the Dennis F7 pump escape and this turntable ladder formed a typical turnout to city centre fires in 1950. (Avon Fire & Rescue Service)

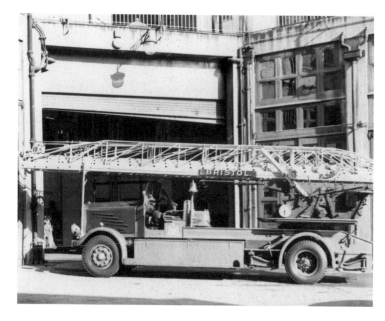

Drill with Dennis F7 pump escape MHW 800 in Bridewell Street yard. With its 900gpm pump it was the most powerful engine in the Bristol Fire Brigade fleet. The appliance had a 162in wheelbase, and the Dennis company soon introduced their F12 model with a shorter (150in) wheelbase. Bristol Fire Brigade bought an F12, registered OHU 229, in 1951. (Mrs Sheila Hunt)

The fire station at Stoke Hill, originally occupied by Canadian firefighters, later served as a training centre for NFS recruits. Bristol Fire Brigade continued to carry out recruit training there. An Austin escape carrier with front-mounted Barton pump is in the foreground, and an Austin heavy unit GLE 900 is on the upper level in front of the appliance garage during a recruits' drill. (Avon Fire & Rescue Service)

In the early 1950s a greater emphasis was placed on fire prevention than had been the case in the past. Bristol Fire Brigade regularly mounted exhibitions as part of an annual nationwide campaign, usually held for a week in the autumn, to make everyone more aware of fire safety. This stand was at the city's museum. (Fred Hooper)

On 6 September 1951, while a cargo of oil was being pumped ashore from the MV *Fort Christina* into a storage tank at the Regent Oil Company's compound at Avonmouth Docks, there was an explosion followed by a fire in the tank. Bristol Fire Brigade, alerted shortly before 3 p.m., initially sent a pump escape, foam tender and wireless car from Station 3, Avonmouth, and the fireboat *Endres Gane*. (Avon Fire & Rescue Service)

The fire spread rapidly to involve twelve tanks containing almost 4 million gallons of oil, and soon reinforcements from the other five fire stations in the city were called in. Here cooling jets are being applied to unaffected tanks. Station 3's Ford wireless car is in the foreground. (Avon Fire & Rescue Service)

Senior officers soon realised that Bristol Fire Brigade could not contain the fire and instructed control room staff to seek outside help. Crews from other brigades were called in and by 9 p.m. 150 firemen with thirty pumps were at the fire. Among the reinforcements was a crew from Station A9 Keynsham of Somerset Fire Brigade with their 1940 Leyland limousine pump EYD 586, seen here. Note the discarded empty foam canisters on the right. (Avon Fire & Rescue Service)

That night, when flames rose hundreds of feet into the air, the sky was lit up as if by a huge torch. There were now enough firemen in attendance to give some of the Bristol crews a break, and progress was made in containing the fire. Then at 4.35 a.m. the roof blew off another tank and flames spreading from it sent firemen running for their lives. Much hose and other pieces of equipment were destroyed. (Avon Fire & Rescue Service)

By daybreak the fire was national news and London newspapers hired light aircraft to fly reporters and cameramen, at some risk, low over the scene. Dramatic pictures and reports appeared on front pages. This view gives a good indication of the size of the fire and the surrounding risks. Eventually twenty-six No.10 foam-making branches supported by thirty cooling jets were used in a concentrated attack to extinguish the fire. Two employees of Regent Oil died in the initial explosion. (*Bristol Evening Post and Press*)

*Right:* A major obstacle to the firefighters was the railway alongside the burning tanks. Pumps and hose-laying lorries could not be driven here and all hoses had to be run out by hand. Almost twenty miles of hose were used altogether and some of it was destroyed in the night-time explosion. (Avon Fire & Rescue Service)

*Below:* Altogether 853 firefighters from twenty-four brigades with sixty pumps and other appliances attended and the firefighters worked in relays of 200 or so at a time. It took thirty-eight hours to finally extinguish the fire. Armed forces personnel also provided back up, fetching and carrying equipment. More than 50,000 gallons of foam-making compound was brought in, much of it in 2-gallon cans. Here naval ratings take a well-earned break. (*Bristol Evening Post and Press*)

While a Shell-Mex Leyland Comet road tanker was delivering petrol to M. & M. Mart Garage in the St Paul's area of Bristol on 24 November 1951 there was an explosion that demolished the three-storey building. Bristol Fire Brigade responded initially with two pumps and a foam tender, and here the Leyland pump HHT 183 is towing the tanker away from the collapsed building. (Avon Fire & Rescue Service)

Casualties were trapped in the building and reinforcing appliances (including the emergency tender) were called. While cooling jets were applied to nearby properties rescue work started, but progress was slow because of the risk of further collapse. It took five hours to locate and release the last of those trapped. Doctors were in attendance and a fleet of eight ambulances took casualties to hospital. (Avon Fire & Rescue Service)

*Above:* The street was busy with Saturday morning shoppers when the explosion occurred shortly after 11.30, but only one passer-by died. However, there were ten other fatalities, including the two owners of M. & M. Mart Garage and members of their family who lived on the premises. Two employees, a customer, the tenant of a flat above the business and the two-man crew of the road tanker also died. (Avon Fire & Rescue Service)

*Right:* A subsequent public enquiry revealed many shortcomings by M. & M.'s management in the storage of petrol. The explosion was thought to have been caused by petrol vapour from an overfilled storage tank under the building spreading through the basement and being ignited by an unprotected solid fuel stove in an adjoining room. (Avon Fire & Rescue Service)

There was another major fire in the high-risk district of St Paul's when this night-time fire broke out at Ackland and Pratten's paper bag factory in Cave Street on 24 March 1952. Firefighters with six pumps and two turntable ladders used sixteen jets and two turntable ladder monitors to extinguish the fire. Lack of fire breaks within the building contributed to it being extensively damaged and much valuable stock was lost. (Avon Fire & Rescue Service)

In the same way that reinforcements from many fire brigades came to assist their Bristol colleagues at the Avonmouth oil fire in September 1951, so Bristol was one of many brigades to send help to East Anglia in the aftermath of the devastating floods of February 1953 when at least 256 people died. Station Officer Prudhoe (ninth from left) led a group of twenty-four firemen with six pumps from Bristol as part of a larger contingent of 120 firemen with thirty pumps from the south-west. (Fred Hooper)

The Bristol men spent eight days at Southwold, near Lowestoft, sleeping at night on the floor of a church hall. Here a Bristol crew (right) work alongside a Somerset crew from Bridgwater pumping out floodwater. Altogether they pumped about 6 million gallons and also cleared houses that had been inundated with mud and shingle. (Fred Hooper)

In 1951 the Government stipulated that all local fire authorities had to submit plans to replace worn-out fire appliances by the end of 1954. Bristol's plan was to replace two Leyland pump escapes that were more than twenty years old and two wartime water tenders. This new Dennis F15 water tender RAE 267 was allocated in 1953 to Station 6, Speedwell Road, covering the eastern side of Bristol. (Keith Wardell Collection)

In the same year Station 5, Ashton Drive, covering the southern side of Bristol, received this Bedford water tender RHT 553. Both stations provided fire cover to rural areas on parts of the Bristol boundary where water supplies were sometimes limited. Appliances such as this Bedford carrying 400 gallons of water were invaluable. (Keith Wardell Collection)

Other Bristol fire stations had to wait longer for modern appliances and this wartime water tender based on an Austin chassis continued to operate from Station 2, Stoke Hill, until 1957. (Avon Fire & Rescue Service)

At the same time the main appliance at Station 2 was this 1933 Leyland pump escape HY 9756. The hand-operated bell is the only emergency warning device. There are no sirens or flashing beacons, nor does the appliance have a radio. The Leyland and the Austin were both replaced by a single Bedford water tender escape, YHU 265, in 1957. (Avon Fire & Rescue Service)

Less than five years after the end of the Second World War the Government re-established the Auxiliary Fire Service (AFS) but, with the anticipated risk of nuclear warfare, the AFS was to be organised into large, self-contained columns that would stay outside the major urban areas. They would only move in after an attack when it was thought safe to do so. Here an AFS column comprising mostly ex-NFS vehicles is on the move near Bristol. (Avon Fire & Rescue Service)

The Bristol AFS contingent trained regularly with Bristol Fire Brigade and formed part of a column alongside AFS colleagues from Gloucestershire and Somerset. Here appliances from the column are gathered in the Wine Street car park, Bristol, during Exercise Vanguard in October 1953. The car park is on the site of buildings destroyed during the Blitz in the winter of 1940–1941. (Avon Fire & Rescue Service)

Communications were vital to the AFS
mobile columns, each of which contained
thirty pumps as well as special appliances.
Motorcyclists attached to the column carried
messages but radio equipment was also used.
Here AFS women radio operators take part
in Exercise Vanguard in central Bristol. (Fred
Hooper)

The pumps of the AFS column come together
in Bristol docks at the end of Exercise
Vanguard and are able to draw on substantial
supplies of water in the dock basin. The old
ex-NFS heavy units, towing vehicles and
trailer pumps would soon be replaced by new
Bedford 900gpm pumps, with enclosed six-
man cabs. (Fred Hooper)

*Left:* Escape drill at Station 4, Brislington, 1954. The station was in an eighteenth-century building, Hemplow House, requisitioned as an AFS station early in the Second World War. Garages to accommodate fire appliances were built in the garden. By 1954 it was overdue for replacement, but CFO Kirkup's plans to do so were frustrated by the national economic situation and it remained in use until December 1962, by which time CFO Kirkup's successor Kenneth Holland described it as 'the worst fire station in the country'. (Fred Hooper)

*Below:* The station's main appliance was this 1937 Leyland pump escape DHY 496. The crew manned, as an alternative appliance, an ex-NFS Fordson water tender GLW 37. Also based at the station was a Fordson hose-laying lorry FYY 320. (Fred Hooper)

A new Bedford water tender escape 150 BHW was allocated to Station 4 in 1957. It was able to combine the roles of the Leyland pump escape and the Fordson water tender. The former became second pump at Bridewell Street Fire Station and the latter was scrapped. The Bedford is seen here at the new Station 4 which was opened at Clothier Road on the Brislington Trading Estate in December 1962. (Keith Wardell Collection)

Among other replacements as part of the 1951 plan were two Bedford pump escapes with bodywork by Oldland Motor Bodies Ltd. Here CFO Kirkup is seen with UHT 994, allocated to Station 5 in 1955. A similar appliance VHY 436 went to Station 3, Avonmouth, in 1956. Alongside UHT 994 stands a Bedford foam tender THU 700, also with Oldland bodywork and also allocated to Station 3. (Avon Fire & Rescue Service)

# THE THREE IN ONE APPLIANCE

## 1 PUMP ESCAPE
## 2 WATER TENDER
## 3 FOAM TENDER

Bedford TRIPLE PURPOSE Fire Appliance. Dennis 500 G.P.M. pump. Wynn Hose Reel Pump. Twin hose reels in lockers. 400 gallons water. 50 gallons foam. Merryweather all steel escape. Prestage power take off.

Pump Escape — Water Tender — Foam Tender
All in one.

*Inquiries Invited*

# OLDLAND MOTOR BODY BUILDERS LTD.

## VICTORIA WORKS, OLDLAND COMMON, BRISTOL
### TELEPHONE BITTON 2132

The Oldland company placed this full-page advertisement in the *Fire Protection Year Book and Directory* for 1958. It featured YHU 265 which was identical in specification to 150 BHW and was allocated to Station 2 at Stoke Hill. But the advertisement did not apparently yield more orders for major fire appliances and the company reverted to basic commercial vehicle body-building. (Author's Collection)

# five

# New Fire
# Stations
# 1959–1974

In 1949 CFO Kirkup had stated that all Bristol's fire stations except Bridewell Street were unsatisfactory. The small station at Green Lane, Avonmouth, had room for only two major appliances, as seen here. Firemen had to run across the busy A4 road to reach the other appliances (like the foam tender) that were kept in a bus garage. (Avon Fire & Rescue Service)

With the slowing of Bristol's fire station building programme after the opening of the new Station 6 at Speedwell Road at the end of 1951, it was not until 1958 that a new five-bay station opened in St Andrew's Road, Avonmouth, to replace the one at Green Lane. The frontage of the new station is seen decorated for an open day in 1959. (Author's Collection)

*Right:* Rescue drill with the 1936 Merryweather turntable ladder CAE 965 during the 1959 open day at the new Avonmouth Fire Station. The appliance was withdrawn from service later that year and the ladders were transferred to a new AEC Mercury chassis with enclosed cab. The ladders were also converted from mechanical to hydraulic operation. (Author's Collection)

*Below:* AEC Mercury/Merryweather turntable ladder 70 GHW, delivered in 1960, is seen here carrying the ladder set from CAE 965. As the newest turntable ladder in the Bristol fleet it went to Station 1, Bridewell Street, with the 1942 Dennis/Merryweather GLW 424 going to Station 6, Speedwell Road, and the 1938 Albion/Merryweather FHT 674 to Station 3, Avonmouth. (Richard Tazewell)

The watch room at Avonmouth Fire Station. It was connected to a number of Gamewell fire alarm points around the docks. These remained in use after the rest of Bristol Fire Brigade's Gamewell street fire alarms were superseded by police telephone pillars in 1934. There was also a direct telephone line to the fireboat berth at Royal Edward Dock. A panel shows the location of shipping in the docks area. (Fred Hooper)

With increasing demand for rescue work in the 1960s, especially as the motorway network developed, in 1968 Bristol Fire Brigade commissioned this Land Rover rescue tender NHY 999F for Avonmouth Fire Station. The brigade also upgraded four pumps so that each now carried portable hydraulic lifting and spreading gear. Their crews were issued with fluorescent jackets to wear when attending road traffic emergency calls. (Avon Fire & Rescue Service)

Although Bristol Fire Brigade vacated Station 2, Stoke Hill, in March 1959 on the expiry of the lease, the new Station 2 at Southmead Road, seen here, was not ready until early in 1960. In the interim the station's Bedford water tender escape, YHU 265, was based at Station 3 and can be seen at the right in the photograph on page 102. (Dave Boulter MBE)

CFO Kirkup did not live to see the official opening of the new Station 2 on 5 May 1960. He died in April 1960, three months before he was due to retire at the age of sixty after thirty-eight years' service. His funeral was held at Canford Cemetery, Bristol, where his coffin, borne on the Leyland DHY 496, passes a guard of honour. (Fred Hooper)

Among the Second World War appliances that gave many years' sterling service was this 1942 Bedford emergency tender GLY 312, converted by the NFS from a Civil Defence heavy rescue unit. It was based at Station 1, Bridewell Street, and was manned by the crew of the station's second pump. (Avon Fire & Rescue Service)

GLY 312 was replaced in 1961 by Bedford 190 LHY which was equipped with a built-in generator to operate floodlighting and power tools. It also carried oxyacetylene cutting equipment and heavy lifting gear as well as breathing and resuscitation apparatus. (Avon Fire & Rescue Service)

Fire at A.G. Shortman & Co., toy and stationery wholesalers, St James Square, May 1961.
Fire spread rapidly among the contents. Six pumping appliances, three from Station 1, two
from Station 5 and one from Station 2 attended. Five jets were used to extinguish the
outbreak. Bristol Fire Brigade's full attendance is seen in the photograph below. (Avon Fire
& Rescue Service)

Three of the six appliances are twenty or more years old, the oldest being the 1933
Leyland HY 9756 running as a reserve pump at Station 5. Two Humber wireless cars
are also present. At this time only five out of eleven of the brigade's first line pumping
appliances carried two-way radio, so the five wireless cars in the fleet often provided vital
communication links in emergency situations. (Avon Fire & Rescue Service)

The modernisation of Bristol Fire Brigade's appliance fleet continued in 1962 with the delivery of this Bedford pump 999 PHY with bodywork by Carmichael of Worcester. It replaced the Leyland HHT 183 as the first pump at Station 1, Bridewell Street. Ten more new major appliances as well as ancillary vehicles would be given 999 registration numbers over the following six years. (Keith Wardell Collection)

Two similar Bedford pumps followed in 1963, with bodywork by Hampshire Car Bodies (HCB) of Totton, Southampton. 999 SHU went to Station 3 and 999 SHY to Station 1. Both had high-pressure hose reels fitted with fog nozzles capable of operating at 350 pounds per square inch (psi). Bedford/HCB hose reel tender 999 RHY replaced a 1942 Austin K2 at Station 1. (Avon Fire & Rescue Service/HCB Angus Archive)

Station 5 at Ashton Drive covering the southern parts of Bristol was built by NFS personnel in 1943. It was not designed for long-term use and was scheduled for replacement by the end of 1954. However, it was not until 1964 that a new four-bay fire station in Hartcliffe Way took its place. In this view of Ashton Drive Bedford pump escape UHT 994 and Bedford water tender RHT 553 are clearly visible. (Fred Hooper)

Station 5, Hartcliffe Way, opened on 28 May 1964. It was designed by the City Architect Mr Albert H. Clarke and completed the ring of five new fire stations built around the city over a fourteen-year period since 1951, leaving only the replacement of Station 1 and HQ at Bridewell Street to complete the building modernisation programme. (Dave Boulter MBE)

Humber 4 x 4 recovery vehicle CAC 572B was acquired in 1964 and based at Station 1, Bridewell Street. It replaced a Dodge JHW 567 that had been converted from one of Bristol's ambulances in 1952. (Robert Bonner)

When Bristol Fire Brigade invited tenders for the supply of a new water tender escape only Dennis Brothers of Guildford were able to meet the specifications. They delivered this F34 model, allocated to Station 5, in 1965. With a Rolls-Royce B81 eight-cylinder petrol engine and automatic gear box the appliance had a top speed of 60mph and could accelerate to 40mph in twenty seconds. (Robert Bonner)

Annual Home Office inspection of Bristol Fire Brigade, October 1965, at Station 2, Southmead, is carried out by Her Majesty's Inspector of Fire Services Albert Thomas (left). He started his fire service career in Bristol in 1927 and was one of eight members of Bristol Fire Brigade who received the George Medal for gallantry at the Pembroke Docks oil fire in August 1940. He joined the Home Office Inspectorate in 1949 after serving as the Chief Fire Officer of Wiltshire Fire Brigade. (Fred Hooper)

Station Officer Ivor Taylor (left) and members of Bristol Fire Brigade's first-aid team. The team won the Fire Brigades National First Aid Competition on several occasions and in 1969, representing all the fire brigades of Great Britain, gained first place in the St John Ambulance Association Grand Prior's Trophy competition in London. (Avon Fire & Rescue Service)

Councillor Roy Willmott, Chairman of the Fire Brigade Committee, presents the
Bristol Fire Brigade Inter-Station Efficiency Shield to Station Officer George Horton of
Station 1 in December 1966. The shield was awarded annually, starting in 1955, to the
station achieving the highest marks over a number of tests including drills, turnouts and
technical knowledge. (Fred Hooper)

Just visiting! A Dennis 'N' model pump dating from the First World War is seen at
Bridewell Street in the late 1960s, with a crew in period uniforms on a charity fund-
raising run. It is identical to the Dennis pumps purchased by Bristol Fire Brigade between
1914 and 1917. Some of them were based during the early 1930s in the appliance room
seen in the background. (Author's Collection)

*Right:* A crowd on the Union Street bridge watch a dramatic fire on 12 May 1966 at Fairfax House, a CRS department store in the Broadmead shopping centre. The seven-storey building was 700ft long but it was also only 45ft wide at its narrowest point. All 800 occupants left safely when the fire was discovered shortly after 12.30 p.m. Fire crews from Station 1 are tackling the fire from the lower level of Fairfax Street. (Avon Fire & Rescue Service)

*Below:* Crews from Stations 5 and 6, responding five minutes later to the message 'Make pumps six – building well alight', had the advantage of tackling the fire from the higher road level of Newgate on the opposite side of the building. The Dennis F34 water tender is seen here and two turntable ladders were used in Fairfax Street. The initial fire spread was rapid, but damage was limited to parts of the fifth and sixth floors of the store. (Avon Fire & Rescue Service)

Another fire in the Broadmead shopping centre but this time with no danger to customers or staff as the outbreak occurred shortly after the Freeman, Hardy & Willis shoe shop had closed for the day on 31 January 1967. The first appliances from Station 1 to attend included Bedford/HCB pump 999 SHY and AEC/Merryweather turntable ladder 70 GHW. (Avon Fire & Rescue Service)

Fire spread rapidly through the second and third floors. The number of pumps attending was increased to four and the breathing apparatus (BA) tender was requested. Here BA wearers are seen at the ground floor entrance. With the use of six BA sets, three jets and two hose reel jets, the fire was quickly brought under control and the stop message was sent forty-five minutes after the initial call had been received. (*Bristol Evening Post & Press*)

Another serious fire broke out early on the morning of 30 April 1967 at W.A. Davies, furniture manufacturers, in the high-risk area of St Paul's. Fire crews with five pumps and two turntable ladders used fourteen jets to extinguish the outbreak. The factory of three floors and basement was severely damaged. (Avon Fire & Rescue Service)

There were casualties when an explosion followed by fire occurred at Springfields Ltd oil merchants, Cole Road, St Philips, on 4 July 1967. Both of Bristol Fire Brigade's foam carriers attended along with five pumps while 400 gallons of foam compound were used to supply the three foam jets used to extinguish the fire. Three of Springfields' employees were injured, one fatally. (Avon Fire & Rescue Service)

A joint drill involving two of Bristol Fire Brigade's three turntable ladders. The 1938 Albion Merryweather FHT 674 suffered a major mechanical breakdown while responding to a fire call on 16 February 1965 and was withdrawn from service. It was eventually replaced in 1967 by an ERF/Simon 65ft hydraulic platform (HP) KHY 999E which was allocated to Station 6. (Avon Fire & Rescue Service)

The HP is seen here in action at a church fire in the Russell Town district, showing how the articulated booms allow close access to roofs. HPs gained greatly in popularity with fire brigades throughout the country in the late 1960s. Bristol Fire Brigade purchased a second one in 1973 but continued to operate two turntable ladders as well. (Avon Fire & Rescue Service)

Although the Government had indicated its support in 1967 for the ongoing work of Civil Defence and Auxiliary Fire Service training, local authorities received a memorandum from the Home Office in February 1968 stating that all such training would cease on 31 March 1968. It was a bitter disappointment to all involved and this final parade of Bristol AFS members was held at Station 6. (Author's Collection)

Bristol's Lord Mayor, the Reverend F.C. Vyvyan-Jones talks to a member of Bristol AFS during the final parade. To the right of the Lord Mayor is CFO Fred Revelle whose own fire service career started with Bristol AFS in 1938. He was also one of the eight men from Bristol to receive the George Medal after the Pembroke Docks oil fire in 1940. (Author's Collection)

Bristol Fire Brigade's appliance replacement programme stalled in the mid-1960s. With no suitable Bedford chassis available for dual-purpose appliances and only a single Dennis purchased in 1965, a second-hand Leyland Comet LUE 474 was purchased from Warwickshire Fire Service and used as a reserve pump escape, pending the choice of a new supplier for replacement appliances. LUE 474 is seen here at Station 4, Brislington. (Ian Moore)

The Leyland Comet remained in the Bristol fleet for only four years and photographs of it in action are rare, but it is seen here at a fire in a property awaiting demolition on the edge of the Broadmead shopping area. A decision was made to purchase dual-purpose appliances with ERF chassis and bodywork by HCB. Two were delivered in 1968 and four more followed by the end of 1971. (Bob Vandereyt)

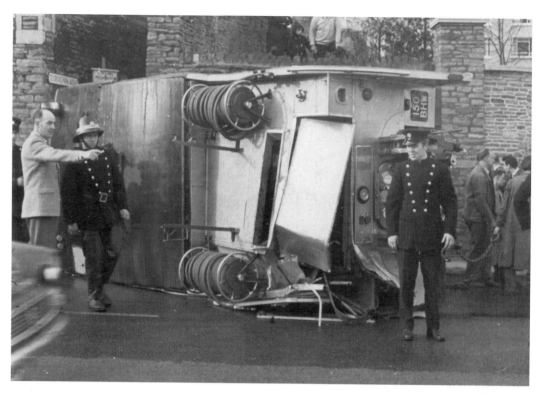

Before the deliveries could even start the fleet was reduced when the Bedford water tender escape 150 BHW overturned in April 1968 while responding from Station 4 to a fire call. Fortunately there were no serious injuries to the crew but the eleven-year-old appliance was written-off. DCFO Basil Roberts (left, in civilian clothing) directs recovery operations. (Avon Fire & Rescue Service)

Another loss occurred in 1970 when the Bedford pump 999 PHY, responding from Station 1 on a fire call, was involved in a road traffic collision. Fortunately, once again there were no serious injuries to crew members, but the damaged appliance was scrapped. (Avon Fire & Rescue Service)

The first two ERF/HCB appliances, RAE 278G and RHT 999G, were allocated to Stations 5 and 6 respectively and the next two, VHU 174H and VHU 175H, went to Stations 3 and 2 in 1970. Although all four operated initially as water tender escapes they could run equally well as water tenders. This gave operational flexibility so that their roles could be switched easily. VHU 174H is seen here at Station 3 shortly after delivery. (Robert Bonner)

The ERF company had designed a chassis specifically for fire appliances but insufficient sales led to a substantial price rise. Bristol Fire Brigade switched to the cheaper option of a Dodge commercial vehicle chassis but kept HCB as body builders. A new feature was a tilting cab to allow easier access to the road engine for maintenance. Dodge/HCB BHY 747 J was allocated to Station 6 as a water tender escape. ERF RHT 999G became the station's water tender. (Author's Collection)

*Right:* Dodge water tender DAE 621K and Dennis F12 pump escape OHU 229 in action at a fire at Haymarket Stores, Ashley Road, Bristol, in September 1971. A woman suffered fatal injuries when she jumped from a second-floor window before the arrival of the brigade. Four other occupants escaped from the first floor via the shop blind and a nearby lamp post. (*Bristol Evening Post and Press*)

*Below:* The last Christmas at Bridewell Street. Members of Red Watch are seen here in front of the appliance room on 24 December 1972. Behind them are Dodge/HCB water tender escape AHU 851J and ERF/HCB water tender DAE 621K. The move to Temple Back in February 1973 would sever a ninety-five-year link with the Bridewell Street site. (Bob Gee)

*Above:* The Control Room at Bridewell Street in 1972 – Control Operator Bob Vandereyt (left) and Senior Control Operator Cyril Stanley. Note the open occurrence book at the right-hand end of the desk. This pattern of book was in use at the time of the Blitz fires in the early 1940s and its style remained unaltered for more than thirty years. It was a daily log and details of all emergency calls were recorded in it. (*Bristol Evening Post and Press*)

*Above:* The nine-bay appliance room housed three front-line pumping appliances and a reserve, two aerial appliances, an emergency tender and a recovery vehicle. All doors to the appliance room were operated electronically and were capable of being opened or closed either individually or from overriding switches in the control room. (Author's Collection)

*Right:* The two aerial appliances were Dodge/Simon 85ft HP FHY 197K and AEC/Merryweather TL PAE 999F. It was possible to crew both appliances simultaneously as the fireboat *Pyronaut* was not replaced when it was withdrawn from service in January 1973. Personnel released from fireboat duties were then available to crew the HP. (*Bristol Evening Post and Press*)

*Opposite below:* Aerial view of the new Headquarters and Central Fire Station, Temple Back. Building work started in April 1970 and the complex became fully operational on 18 February 1973. Allowances had been made for the anticipated changes of 1 April 1974 when Bristol Fire Brigade was to become part of the new County of Avon Fire Brigade. For example, the new control room console had facilities to mobilise up to twenty-six fire stations. (Author's Collection)

Dodge/Simon HP FHY 197K is seen here at work at a fire at the Robin Hood's Retreat public house in the Gloucester Road area of Bristol. The city's Public Protection Committee had expressed great satisfaction with the performance of the 65ft HP delivered in 1967 and decided to buy this larger 85ft model. Delivery was delayed until 1973 as it was too big for the appliance room bays at Bridewell Street. (Avon Fire & Rescue Service)

During its ninety-six-year history Bristol Fire Brigade dealt with many ship fires and explosions. In early times these mainly involved vessels in the city docks but after Avonmouth Docks were developed the majority of ship-related incidents occurred there. This fire on 18 October 1972 on board the *City of Gloucester* required six pumps, a foam carrier, a fireboat, a control unit and hi-ex foam unit. (Avon Fire & Rescue Service)

Fire in a cargo of jute on board MV *Mergui* at Avonmouth Docks on 5 April 1973 spread to crew quarters and stores where oil ignited and exploded. Described as the worst ship fire in Bristol for twenty years, the outbreak was fought by eighty firemen, some from Gloucestershire Fire Service, with twelve pumps, a foam tender, foam carrier, a fireboat, a hi-ex foam unit, an emergency tender, a control unit and an HP. This was the first incident attended by the new 85ft HP. It entered service only the day before. (Avon Fire & Rescue Service)

The Avonmouth fireboat *Endres Gane* was decommissioned in 1967 and replaced by *Aquanaut* built by the Thames Launch Co. Ltd of Twickenham. The vessel was of unusual appearance, being square-ended fore and aft, but it had the power to deliver up to 6,000gpm of firefighting foam or 2,500gpm of water. For salvage work the vessel had a pumping capacity of 2,200gpm. It attended both the *City of Gloucester* and *Mergui* fires. (Avon Fire & Rescue Service)

Still with us! A considerable number of appliances from Bristol Fire Brigade's fleet have been preserved. Some are in full working order while others await restoration. The oldest preserved appliance is the 1931 Leyland Lioness HY 1801 owned by David Berry of Swindon. It is in full working order and regularly appears at vintage vehicle events. (Fire Fotos, Burley, Hants)

Work in progress. The 1937 Leyland DHY 496 was stored in a barn on a Cornish farm for more than twenty years following its disposal by Bristol Fire Brigade in 1969. It was acquired, as seen here, by Richard Aston of Newbury, Berkshire, in 2005 for restoration. A third Leyland, the 1932 pump escape HY 4979, is owned by Nick Baker of Gillingham, Dorset. This appliance should also be seen at summer events in the future. (Richard Aston)

The 1940 Leyland/Merryweather turntable ladder GHW 415 was transferred by the NFS from Bristol to Salisbury, passing on 1 April 1948 to the newly formed Wiltshire Fire Brigade and continuing in service at Salisbury Fire Station until 1968. The appliance remains in Wiltshire in the ownership of Mr Keith Miller at Westbury. Other turntable ladders preserved are the 1938 Albion/Merryweather FHT 674, the 1942 Dennis/Merryweather GLW 424, the 1960 AEC/Merryweather 70 GHW and the 1968 AEC/Merryweather PAE 999F. (Clive Shearman)

Finally there are a group of appliances from the late 1960s and early 1970s, including two Land Rover pumps UHW 481/2 H, Bedford Chemical Incident Unit BHW 486J, two water tender escapes, Dodge/Jennings HAE 418K and this ERF/HCB DAE 621K, owned by Roger Chambers of Bristol. (Roger Chambers)

# Other titles published by Tempus

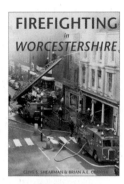

## Firefighting in Worcestershire
CLIVE S. SHEARMAN & BRIAN A.E. CORNISH

From the earliest times the county of Worcestershire regularly suffered from the ravages of fire, but since the government decree of 1666 that each parish should have a fire engine Worcestershire has been fortunate to have some protection. By the 1900s each town had its own brigade and inside these pages are the pictures and stories that will stir the memories of firefighting enthusiasts and locals alike.

978 07524 3166 6

## Firefighting in Kent
ROGER C. MARDON & JOHN A. MEAKINS

Organised firefighting came to Britain with the Romans when they landed at Richborough, Kent, in AD 43. The county has been at the forefront of developments in the field ever since. Firefighting was initially a community affair and it was not until the nineteenth century that fire brigades were formed in Kent. With the use of over 200 photographs covering every aspect of the fire brigade, this book is a must for both local historians and firefighting enthusiasts.

978 07524 3260 1

## Northumberland Fire & Rescue Service
RON HENDERSON

The population of Northumberland is greatly dependent on the efficiency and professionalism of its fire brigade for ensuring the safety of both residents and visitors. Charting the changes in the service over the last sixty years, with the use of over 150 photographs and detailed text, Ron Henderson has given us a comprehesive portrayal of a service on which we all depend.
978 07524 3540 4

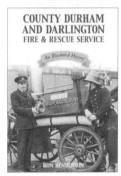

## County Durham and Darlington Fire & Rescue Service
RON HENDERSON

The County Durham and Darlington Fire and Rescue Service affords fire protection to a population of just over half a million people within its borders of Cleveland and North Yorkshire to the south, Cumbria to the west and Tyne & Wear and Northumberland to the north. Featuring over 150 photographs of the County Durham fire service since 1948, Ron Henderson has created an evocative record of its post-war history.

978 07524 4179 5

If you are interested in purchasing other books published by Tempus, or in case you have difficulty finding any Tempus books in your local bookshop, you can also place orders directly through our website

**www.tempus-publishing.com**